First published in the UK in 1998 by

Belitha Press Limited
London House, Great Eastern Wharf,
Parkgate Road, London SW11 4NQ

ISBN 1 85561 797 8

British Library Cataloguing in Publication Data for this book
is available from the British Library.

Printed in Singapore

Editor: Stephanie Bellwood
Designer: Guy Callaby
Picture researcher: Diana Morris
Illustrator: Richard Prideaux
Consultants: Elizabeth Atkinson
            Susan Daniels, The National Deaf Children's Society
Series consultant: Peter White, BBC Disability Affairs Correspondent
With thanks to the RNID

Picture acknowledgements:
Julian Baum/SPL: 28tr. BBC Education: 5c. Elie Bernager/Getty Images: 8t. Giles
Bernard/Photofusion: 13t. British Council: 9b. British Museum: 18b. E.T. Archive: 26b
Beethoven House, Bonn. Express & Star, Wolverhampton: 11t. Isabelle Foulkes © Deaf
Aardvark: 21t. Getty Images: 9t, 26t, 27t. Hearing Dogs for Deaf People: 19. Peter
Heimsath/RexFeatures: 27b. James King-Holmes/SPL: 11b. Zigy Kaluzny/Getty Images:
17t. Sandra Lousada/Collections: front cover. Astrid & Hans-Frieder Michler/SPL: 7b.
Lawrence Migdale/Getty Images: 14t. Laurence Monneret/SPL: 12t. Maggie Murray/Format:
12b, 15b. NASA: 28t. Anne Nielson/Getty Images: 16t. North Wind Picture Archives: 8b.
Nottingham Group Ltd: 16b. Gary Parker/SPL: 10c. Ulrike Preuss/Format: 14b, 29t. RNID:
4b Friends for Young Deaf People, 18c, 20b, 22b, 24b, 25t, 25b. Ron Sangha/Getty Images:
6t. Blaire Seitz/SPL: 5t. Jim Selby/SPL: 10t. Jane Shemilt/SPL: 28b. Paula Solloway/Format:
15t. © Sound Seekers: 29c. © Tate Gallery, London: 26c. Telegraph Colour Library: 24t.
Bob Thomas/Getty Images: 4t, 18t. Terry Vine/Getty Images: 20t. Carol Weinberg/BMG: 21c.
John Wender/Collections: 7t. WESCO, Cerizay: 13c. David Young Wolff/Getty Images: 22t.

Words in **bold** are explained in the glossary on pages 30 and 31.

THINK ABOUT

Being
DEAF

Maggie Woolley

Belitha Press

ABOUT THE AUTHOR

Maggie Woolley began to go deaf while she was at school. Her father was also deaf from childhood.

Maggie campaigned hard for television programmes to be shown with sign language, and she then became the first deaf television presenter in this country. She presented the BBC programme *See Hear* for six years and then became a producer on the programme. In 1988 she became Director of an arts charity for deaf and disabled people called Shape.

Maggie contributes to radio and television programmes and writes for magazines and books. She has two daughters, one of whom is deaf, and she likes gardening and watching football.

Contents

Understanding deafness

Close your eyes and listen. What can you hear?
If you tried to make a list of everything you can
hear it would soon be a very long list indeed.
There are sounds all around you. Even in very
quiet places you can hear things like insects buzzing, the wind rustling the trees,
or aeroplanes far away in the sky. People who are deaf can't hear all these noises.
They have to learn different ways of understanding the world of sound.

How many people are deaf?

One person in every seven
people in Britain becomes deaf.
Most of them lose their hearing
as they grow older. They are
called hard of hearing. One
in every thousand babies
in Britain is born deaf, but
most of them can hear a little.
Hearing children learn how
to speak by listening to their
parents, family and friends.
It can be difficult for deaf
children to learn to speak
because they can't hear their
voice or copy other people.

◀ **These children are both deaf,
but you can't tell from just
looking. They are on an activity
day organized by a charity called
Friends for Young Deaf People.**

Sign language

Some deaf people use a language of their own called British **Sign Language** (BSL). Other countries have their own sign languages too. When these deaf people travel abroad they quickly make friends with other deaf people because sign languages are easier to learn than spoken or written languages. To talk in sign language they use their hands and the expressions on their faces.

▶ Learning to use sign language can be good fun and very useful too.

◀ This television programme is presented in sign language by a deaf man. It helps many deaf people to keep in touch with news and events.

Do deaf people miss out?

If you turn off the sound on your favourite television programme you soon become bored and even annoyed because things don't make sense. You might think that this means deaf people miss out on things like television. But many programmes now have **subtitles** so that deaf people can read what is being said. Some programmes are presented in sign language by deaf people or have **sign language** interpreters at the side of the screen.

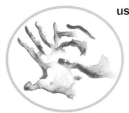

(THINK ABOUT)

Language

You are always using language. Even when you're quiet and on your own, or if you're doing something simple like tying your shoelaces, you are using language to think. Could you make sense of things or think at all without language? Many deaf people use sign language for having conversations with other people, but they think and dream in sign language too.

What is deafness?

Most deaf people have some hearing. Very few are totally deaf. Many people lose their hearing as they grow older, but you can lose your hearing through illness, accidents, explosions or jobs where there is a lot of noise. A few children are born deaf. Doctors don't always know why, but sometimes deafness is **inherited** from one of their parents.

▼ **This diagram shows the parts inside a human ear.**

How the ear works

Sounds go into your **ear** and down a tube called the ear canal. They **vibrate** on the **eardrum**. Next to the eardrum are three little bones called the hammer, the anvil and the stirrup. They are the smallest bones in your body, and they would fit on your little fingernail. These bones pass the vibrations to the **cochlea**. **Nerves** then carry the sound messages to the brain.

anvil

hammer

nerves leading to the brain

cochlea

stirrup

ear canal   eardrum

Different kinds of deafness

Any part of the ear can go wrong, causing different kinds of deafness. A loud sound such as an explosion can puncture the eardrum so that it doesn't vibrate properly. People who work in noisy jobs often lose their hearing. This happens slowly as parts of the ear are damaged by the constant noise.

▲ Workmen wear ear protectors so that their hearing isn't damaged by the sound of loud drills.

How do we know if a baby is deaf?

Babies can be tested soon after they are born to see if they are deaf. Doctors use special equipment to measure how the baby's brain reacts to sounds. Deaf people often can't hear consonant sounds such as 's' and 't', which are higher than vowel sounds such as 'ee' and 'oh'. This means that it is very difficult for them to understand speech.

THINK ABOUT

Sound

What is it like to be deaf? People who are hard of hearing can hear background noise but they can't tell what someone is saying to them. Imagine listening to loud music through headphones and trying to hear someone talking to you at the same time. People who are very deaf use their other senses instead. They watch people's faces and lip-read. They can also tell a lot from vibrations, for example when they are dancing to music.

◀ A baby's hearing can be tested in different ways. The baby's response to this squeaky toy gives the doctor an idea of how much the baby can hear.

A history of deafness

For hundreds of years everyone thought deaf people were stupid because they couldn't speak properly. No-one understood **sign language** or realized that it was a proper language. Hearing people and deaf people couldn't communicate at all. Before modern **hearing aids** were invented it was hard to help deaf children to speak clearly.

Deaf American settlers
In the sixteenth century many English people went to live in America. Some settlers lived on an island called Martha's Vineyard. A few of these people were deaf. Over the years the number of deaf people grew and sign language became a common way of communicating. It was often more useful than speech, when people wanted to call across a crowded room or when they were out fishing.

Deaf and hearing people lived together on Martha's Vineyard. In the twentieth century many islanders moved to the mainland of America, so the deaf community broke up.

Early schools

The first schools for deaf children were set up in the eighteenth century in Britain and Europe. An American called Thomas Gallaudet saw these schools and decided to start a school for deaf children in America. He went back to America with a French man called Laurent LeClerc, who was a deaf teacher. LeClerc taught the teachers to use sign language, and a school was set up in Connecticut.

Children in a biology lesson at a special school for deaf children, in 1908.

A deaf child having a speech class in the 1940s. These lessons were very hard for many children.

Banning sign language

In the nineteenth century and early twentieth century many people thought that deaf children should learn to speak instead of having a language of their own. Sign language was banned in many schools all over the world and deaf teachers lost their jobs. It was a very sad time for many deaf people because without sign language they couldn't learn to read and write properly. Children were punished for using sign language, but they still signed when the teachers weren't looking.

THINK ABOUT

Jobs

Can you imagine how difficult life was for deaf children who weren't allowed to use sign language? They weren't taught much, and they were given dull jobs such as working in a factory, making shoes or sewing clothes. These were very noisy jobs, and so employers used deaf people who wouldn't be distracted by all the noise. This made everyone think that deaf people couldn't do any other kind of work.

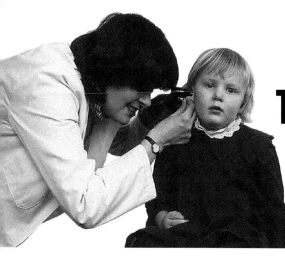

Treatment of deafness

You may see stories in the news about deaf people who have had amazing operations to help them hear again. It's true that some operations help people to hear better, but only a few people ever have perfect hearing again. But there are ways to prevent deafness or to help people to make the most of the hearing they have left.

Glue ear

Children sometimes have a kind of deafness called **glue ear**. Their **ears** become blocked so the child can't hear properly. Sometimes glue ear is cured by placing a **grommet** inside the ear. Glue ear can last a long time, and some children have it again and again.

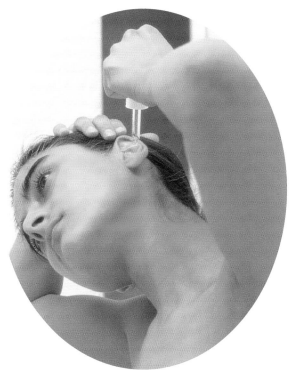

▶ Most of us have been a little bit deaf at one time or another. Having blocked ears is very common. You can put ear drops in your ear using a dropper. They quickly remove the blockage and ease the pain.

THINK ABOUT

Protecting your ears

A lot of deafness can be prevented if people protect their ears. Many people have hearing problems because they have spent too much time listening to very loud music. Even poking your ear can damage it, so be careful!

Wearing a hearing aid

Hearing aids help some deaf people to hear better because they **amplify** sounds. A hearing aid is usually worn behind the person's ear. It has a tiny microphone powered by batteries. A plastic tube goes from the hearing aid to an **earmould** inside the ear. Everyone's ear is a different shape, so a special mould is made to fit inside the ear. Children need new moulds every few months because their ears are still growing.

◀ This boy is enjoying a puppet show with a special sign language toy (see page 16). You can see the boy's earmould, the hearing aid and the wire leading to the batteries.

Operations to help deafness

Eardrums can sometimes be repaired with an operation, and the three bones in the ear can sometimes be replaced with **artificial** bones. People with a badly damaged **cochlea** may have a **cochlear implant** placed under the skin behind the ear. They wear a tiny microphone that picks up sounds. The sounds are turned into electrical signals by a special box called a speech processor. The signals are transmitted into the inner ear and passed along the **nerve**. When the messages reach the brain they give a sensation of sound.

◀ The part of the cochlear implant behind the ear is the microphone. It picks up sounds and sends them to the round piece on the head, which is a transmitter. This sends messages to a receiver inside the head.

At home

If you had a deaf brother or sister, would they be able to join in games or play with your friends? Would they be able to understand what you say to them? There are lots of ways to help deaf children be part of a happy family. After all, they can do everything except hear! Families learn how to communicate so that a deaf child can always join in.

Being part of the family

When there is a deaf person in the family, everyone must remember to include them all the time. Families often chat away while they are preparing a meal or getting ready for school, and a deaf child might find it hard to keep up with the conversation. Everyone must make sure the deaf person knows what's going on. And of course deaf children want a say in decisions such as what to play or what to have for tea.

▲ This deaf girl is reading with her mum. She is profoundly deaf, which means that she can hardly hear at all, even with a hearing aid.

Learning to be helpful

Deaf people need to be able to see you to understand what you are saying or signing. They often like you to touch them gently on the shoulder to attract their attention. When you are walking it's better to stop when you want to talk. Many people have walked into lamp posts because they were talking or signing to a deaf person and not looking where they were going!

You must try to speak clearly to deaf people. Learning sign language can help too.

There are many things on this play mat to look at and pull or squeeze. The clown toy is colourful, with parts to turn and press.

Play time

Deaf babies need lots of toys to keep them interested and **alert**. The best toys are ones that are bright and colourful, with plenty of parts to look at and touch, such as the toys in the photographs above. Toys that move, light up or make noises when the deaf child makes a sound are good too. They help the child to realize when they are making sounds.

THINK ABOUT

Families

Now imagine what it would be like if your mum or dad were deaf. If they used sign language, you could learn how to use it too. This might be very useful to you later in life. Many children of deaf parents have careers as sign language interpreters. Others decide to be actors because they are so confident at communicating by using their movements, gestures and facial expressions.

At school

Think about all the things you hear at school. Even in the playground and when you are having lunch you are using your hearing. Perhaps the only time when things are quiet in school is when the teacher tells everyone to stop talking and concentrate on their work. What would school be like if you were deaf?

These children go to a school for hearing and deaf pupils. Some children wear extra strong hearing aids at school to help them to hear what the teacher says.

Special help for deaf pupils

Nine out of ten deaf children in Britain go to ordinary schools. Some schools have special areas where deaf children work for part of the day with specially-trained teachers. Classes in these areas are very small so that teachers can help each child and make sure that they learn just as much as hearing children in the ordinary classroom. Sometimes teachers wear a microphone so that the children can hear their voice more clearly.

Schools for deaf children

Some children go to special schools where all the children are deaf. Some children prefer this kind of school because they can understand each other by using **sign language**. Some children live a long way from the school so they stay at school all week and go home at weekends.

▼ Do you learn to play musical instruments at school? Deaf children often like music too. This deaf girl plays the recorder at school.

▲ In many special schools all the teachers know how to use sign language. This teacher is deaf, so he has no problem teaching deaf pupils.

Music lessons

Deaf children learn the same subjects at school as hearing children. They even have music lessons. One school for deaf children has its own orchestra. Some deaf children perform songs and plays using sign language.

Feeling lonely

Imagine how confused you would be if you couldn't understand what your teacher and friends were saying. It would be like standing outside watching everything through a window and only being able to guess what people inside were saying. You might feel very cut off and lonely. Why do you think some deaf children like to have deaf and hearing friends who have learned to use sign language? What else could you do to communicate better?

Communication

Deaf babies may have difficulty learning to communicate. They don't speak clearly because they can't hear the noises they are making or the way other people speak. But with the help of **sign language**, **hearing aids** and **lip-reading**, deaf children can learn to communicate just as well as everyone else.

◀ The hands of this big puppet can be moved to teach deaf children sign language. The puppet's mouth and tongue can also be moved to show how basic sounds are formed using lip and tongue positions.

Lip-reading

Many deaf people learn to lip-read because it helps them to understand what hearing people are saying. Lip-reading can be very difficult. Not all sounds are easy to see on someone's lips, and many sounds look the same. Look in a mirror and mouth the sounds 'f' and 'v'. They look very similar, don't they? Now try the sounds 'p', 'b' and 'm'. You can see how easy it is to make mistakes.

These deaf teenagers are using American sign language.

Fingerspelling

Words can also be signed using **fingerspelling**. There is a sign for each letter of the alphabet. Fingerspelling is quick and easy to learn. In Britain people use two hands for fingerspelling, but people in America and many other countries use one hand. You need to know the spoken language of a country to understand their fingerspelling. For example, it's no use learning Japanese fingerspelling if you don't speak any Japanese!

Queen Victoria learned how to fingerspell so that she could talk to a deaf woman called Mrs Tuffield, who ran the local post office.

Sign language

Signing looks very complicated. But sign language is much easier than lip-reading once people know how to use it. It is a proper language, unlike lip-reading where people have to use a lot of guesswork.

When people sign they use their hands, face and the space in front of the top half of their body. Sign languages are different in every country. Even in Britain, sign language isn't always the same. It varies from place to place, just like spoken language, where people from different areas have different accents.

THINK ABOUT

Everyday signs

Can you think of other people who use sign language? In a football match you can see players and coaches signing to each other. Signs are vital to people such as deep sea divers and astronauts. Now think about the signs we use every day, such as nodding, waving and pointing. You can often tell when people are excited, angry or tired by the way they move their hands.

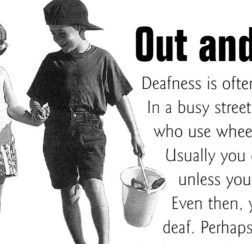

Out and about

Deafness is often called an invisible disability. In a busy street you notice blind people or people who use wheelchairs, but you can't see deafness. Usually you don't realize that people are deaf unless you see them signing to each other. Even then, you can't be sure that they are both deaf. Perhaps one of them can hear and is using **sign language** because the other person is deaf.

Shopping and travelling

As more people learn sign language, deaf people can communicate easier in places like shops and restaurants. More public places are now giving deaf people extra help. At many airports there are staff who have been specially trained to communicate with deaf people. **Sign language interpreters** are trained to work with some deaf people.

A deaf woman (right) uses a sign language interpreter (left) to help at a business meeting.

Using an interpreter

Deaf people enjoy many events with the help of sign language interpreters. The interpreter listens to what is said and **translates** it into sign language. Interpreters also translate sign language into speech. They work in places such as law courts, hospitals and universities.

A sign language interpreter gives deaf people a guided tour around a museum.

Hearing dogs for deaf people

You have probably seen guide dogs helping blind people, but did you know that dogs can be trained to help deaf people too? Young hearing dogs spend a year with a foster family to find out whether they will be good at working for deaf people. They then spend four months at a training centre. When they are trained they are given to a deaf owner.

Hearing dogs help their owners at home and at work. They let their owners know when the phone or doorbell is ringing and even wake them up in the morning when the alarm clock goes off.

This hearing dog is called Kenya. She was rescued from a dogs' home and is now happily settled with her new family.

THINK ABOUT

Using your eyes

In railway stations, airports and many public places, announcements are made over loudspeakers. Deaf people have to look for written information to tell them when a train is due or if it is delayed. When you are in a station or an airport, look out for useful and important notices. Listen to the announcements and check that the same information also appears on computer screens or boards.

Fun and games

Many deaf people who use **sign language** love being together, just like any group who use the same language. There are hundreds of clubs and societies where they meet to relax or enjoy hobbies. Deaf people play all kinds of sports too. When deaf children are learning adventurous activities such as abseiling, rock climbing, canoeing and sailing they need help from someone who can communicate clearly or who knows sign language.

Brian Kokoruwe is one of the fastest deaf 400m runners in Europe. He has competed in the deaf Olympic Games.

Deaf athletics

The deaf Olympic Games are held every four years, and thousands of deaf people travel to support their country. Think how great it must be for deaf athletes to see crowds of people using sign language from all over the world.

You might think that people who are too deaf to hear the starting gun can't be runners. But they can learn to be so aware of the other runners that they spring into action at the same moment as everyone else.

Theatre, art and dance

When deaf people meet to have a good time together, they may sit or stand in a big circle and tell stories in sign language. Funny stories are often popular. A lot of deaf people enjoy acting and performing songs, dance or poetry in sign language. Some deaf people enjoy painting or sculpture. They sometimes use art to express their feelings about deafness.

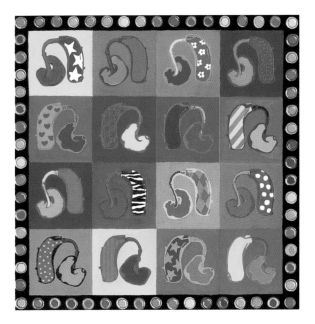

This painting by deaf artist Isabelle Foulkes uses colourful, bold shapes to make hearing aids look cheerful and fun.

Evelyn Glennie plays lots of percussion instruments. These are instruments that are shaken or hit, such as bells or drums.

Making music

Amazingly enough, many deaf people love playing musical instruments. Some people who have a little bit of hearing can hear low notes and feel the way higher notes vibrate. Evelyn Glennie is a musician. She became deaf when she was eight years old, but this did not change her love of music. She works all over the world, playing in orchestras and composing music for television and films.

THINK ABOUT

Free time

Think about things you enjoy doing and work out how a deaf person might enjoy them. Could a deaf person fly an aeroplane or do a parachute jump? You might think that having a holiday abroad could be difficult for deaf people, but everyone has a few problems when they don't understand foreign languages!

Going to work

When deaf people grow up they want to work and earn money, have families of their own and achieve other ambitions. Deaf people are as intelligent as anyone else and they learn skills at school and college. But it can still be difficult for them to find the job they want because employers often think that deaf people will have too many problems at work.

All kinds of jobs

Deaf people have a wider choice of careers than you might think. They might work with other people, become computer experts, or work with their hands. Deaf people can always do a good job as long as everyone else understands their needs and makes an effort to communicate.

▶ Would you like to have a career working outdoors? Leslie is deaf and works in the countryside. His job is to look after large areas of land.

Being a journalist

Deaf people were rejected for many jobs in the past because they couldn't use the telephone. Nowadays there are many other ways of keeping in touch, such as **fax** and **e-mail**. Melissa, who is deaf, is a journalist who has worked for famous magazines such as Vogue. She has a **pager** and a **Minicom**.

▶ Melissa regularly visits clothes shows and writes about new styles and fashions.

Presenting TV programmes

Jackie is deaf and has a **cochlear implant**. She works as a **sign language** presenter on a television programme. Jackie has other career plans too. She is studying at university to be a lawyer.

▲ Jackie works hard to fit in all her studying as well as her job as a television presenter.

THINK ABOUT

Having a career

Everyone thinks about the job they would like to do when they grow up. Are there any jobs that you think a deaf person couldn't do? Deaf people become lawyers, astronomers, models and lorry drivers. In fact, they can do just about every job you can think of apart from being telephone operators. They can't be sound engineers in a film crew either, but they can work in film or television.

Amazing inventions

There are many inventions that help deaf people. Probably the most useful devices are the special telephones that allow deaf people to communicate with everyone else. The first telephone was invented in 1876 by Alexander Graham Bell, a man who was very interested in the human voice. This was partly because his mother and his wife were both deaf. But it wasn't until a hundred years later that telephones were invented for deaf people too.

Helping people to hear better

The loop system helps people who wear **hearing aids** to hear the television or music. A loop is a wire with a microphone near the source of sound. The deaf person turns a switch on their hearing aid and picks up sound from the microphone. Public places such as cinemas, shops and airports often have loops.

Alarms and warnings

Alarm clocks for deaf people can be attached to a lamp that flashes or a pad that **vibrates** when the alarm goes off. Lights in the house can be connected to telephone bells, smoke alarms, baby alarms and doorbells. When an alarm goes off the deaf person is **alerted** by flashing lights.

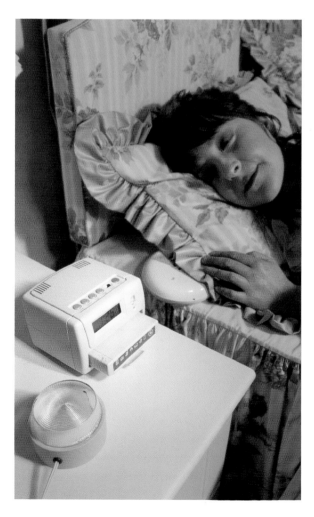

▶ This alarm clock has a light that flashes when the alarm goes off. There is also a round pad that the deaf person puts under their pillow. It vibrates at the same time as the alarm rings.

Nowadays many TV programmes have subtitles. People who work as subtitlers listen to programmes and type in speech and sounds. The words appear at the bottom of the TV screen in different colours.

Special telephones

Most deaf people use telephones called **textphones**. Instead of speaking or listening, they type and read messages on a screen. Deaf people use textphones at home and at work. Places such as shops, banks and public telephones now have textphones.

The Typetalk service

If you want to contact a deaf person who has a textphone, you can use a telephone service called **Typetalk**. An operator types your message and sends it to the deaf person's textphone. They type a reply and the operator reads it out to you.

This is a textphone. The deaf person types a message on to the small screen and sends it to someone. The message is also printed out.

Famous deaf people

Over the years there have been many famous deaf people. The Roman Emperor Hadrian was supposedly so deaf that he had to ride into battle with his hand cupped behind his ear! Some people tried to hide their deafness. Queen Alexandra, the wife of Edward VII, wore elaborate hairstyles and huge hats to cover her **ear trumpets** that were designed to look like jewellery.

Ludwig van Beethoven (1770-1827)

Ludwig van Beethoven was a famous composer, pianist and conductor. From the age of 28 he gradually became deaf. At first he was upset and depressed, but he went on to compose some of his most famous symphonies. By the age of 48 Beethoven was completely deaf.

Deaf artists

There have been many successful deaf artists. Francisco de Goya (1746-1828) was a Spanish painter who became totally deaf after a serious illness. Henri de Toulouse-Lautrec (1864-1901) was a French artist who was **partially** deaf. The English painter Joshua Reynolds (1723-92) lost his hearing in a riding accident. David Hockney (born 1937) is a modern artist who wears **hearing aids** that are as colourful as the pictures he paints.

This painting is a self-portrait by Joshua Reynolds. He has his hand behind his ear to help him hear better.

As Beethoven became deaf he cut himself off from everyone around him. He expressed his thoughts and feelings in the music he wrote.

Thomas Edison (1847-1931)

Thomas Edison is one of the world's most famous inventors. He became deaf when he was a boy. Edison invented the light bulb and more than a thousand gadgets. He also invented the phonograph, the first way of recording and playing sounds, even though he couldn't hear it. He improved Alexander Graham Bell's early telephone too.

World leaders

Quite a few world leaders have been deaf. Sir Winston Churchill, Britain's prime minister during the Second World War and the early 1950s, didn't like people to know that he was hard of hearing. He was very grumpy about it. Two important modern leaders, President Clinton in the USA and President Mandela in South Africa, are also hard of hearing.

▲ Thomas Edison's amazing inventions helped to change the world. Imagine what life would be like without electricity!

(THINK ABOUT)

Fame

Read about other famous people who were deaf. Did being deaf cause them problems or stop them achieving their goals?

▲ Both President Nelson Mandela and President Bill Clinton wear hearing aids. Their hearing aids cannot be seen easily.

Looking to the future

A hundred years ago there were no **hearing aids** and not many people understood **sign language**. There were no special telephones and no help for deaf people in public places. Many things are different now. But what will life be like for deaf people in the next hundred years?

New technology

Hearing aids are being improved all the time. In the future they should give a much better sound quality. The newest hearing aids are small enough to fit inside the **ear**. But they can't be too small or it would be impossible to use the switches.

Work is being done to make hearing aids that have no switches at all and are **implanted** inside people's heads. Scientists are also trying to programme computers to recognize human speech. Perhaps in the future deaf people will have tiny pocket computers that instantly **translate** speech into writing or signing.

Some people already use tiny hearing aids that fit inside the ear canal. The cable sticks out so that the hearing aid can be pulled out.

Future sign language

Over the last century deaf people have developed an international sign language so that they can understand each other at meetings involving several countries. There may soon be sign language television channels. More and more hearing people are learning to sign. There are even university courses in sign language and Deaf Studies. Perhaps in the future all children will learn how to sign at school.

These children are taking part in a sign language class for hearing and deaf children.

A deaf child from Botswana, in Africa, with a special solar-powered hearing aid. It is rechargeable, which means that it doesn't use up expensive batteries.

Could deafness disappear?

Deafness will probably never disappear altogether, but as we understand more about **genes**, it might be possible to help damaged parts of the ear to grow again. Perhaps we will get better at learning what goes wrong with ears so that problems can be dealt with earlier. But whatever exciting possibilities there may be, many deaf people won't want to give up sign language and the enjoyment it gives them.

THINK ABOUT
Know the rules

There are several rules that you must remember when you are talking to a deaf person. Make sure there is light on your face so the deaf person can see it clearly. Either use sign language or gestures and facial expressions to make lip-reading easier. Try to speak clearly, but don't shout. It won't help!

Glossary

alert Paying attention and aware of what's going on.

amplify To make a sound louder. Hearing aids amplify sound for deaf people.

artificial Something that is specially made, not natural.

cochlea A spiral tube in the ear, shaped like a snail shell. Sound vibrations go through the middle ear and into the cochlea. Here they are changed into nerve messages. The messages are then sent to the brain and heard as sound.

cochlear implant A type of hearing aid that can help people who have a damaged cochlea. It is implanted behind the ear with parts in the cochlea. Sounds are turned into electrical signals and passed to the brain through the implant.

ear The ear has three parts. The outer ear is the part you can see and the ear canal. The middle ear contains three tiny bones. The inner ear sorts out sounds for the brain. It includes the cochlea (see diagram on page 6).

eardrum A thin layer of tissue inside the ear that separates the outer ear from the middle ear. Sound vibrates on the eardrum.

earmould The part of a hearing aid that fits in the ear.

ear trumpet An ear trumpet is a long tube that is wide at the end. Some people used ear trumpets before modern hearing aids were invented. They held the trumpet to one ear to help them hear what other people said.

e-mail A way of sending written messages from one computer to another.

fax A quick way of sending letters or important papers. The paper goes through the fax machine and the message is sent down a telephone line to another machine. There the page is printed out.

fingerspelling This is also called the manual alphabet. There is a simple hand symbol for each letter of the alphabet. You can use these symbols to spell out words and names.

genes Parts of cells in the body that make each person different. Everyone inherits their genes from their parents.

glue ear Thick liquid behind the eardrum that blocks the ear. This stops the person from hearing properly. It's just like trying to hear with your fingers stuck in your ears. Children are more likely to have glue ear than adults.

grommet A grommet is a small tube that can help to cure glue ear. A small cut is made in the eardrum to let the liquid drain out, then the grommet is put in to let air in the ear and keep it healthy.

hearing aid A device that makes sounds louder for people who are partially deaf or hard of hearing. Sound is picked up by a microphone and passed into the ear through a small tube. The important thing to know about hearing aids is that they only amplify sounds that the person can already hear. This means that they can be useful but they can't help anyone hear perfectly.

implant To put something inside the body.

inherited Passed down from a parent. Children inherit looks from parents and other family members. They can also inherit disabilities such as deafness if they have deaf parents.

lip-reading Watching a person's lips to try and work out what they are saying. Some deaf people learn to lip-read. They may also use a hearing aid to help them tell what is being said.

Minicom A textphone with a keyboard and a small screen.

nerves Nerves are tiny, thin threads in our bodies that carry messages to the brain.

pager A small machine that has a screen where messages are received. People speak the message to a telephone operator or send typed messages from a textphone.

partially Partly, not totally. People with partial deafness have some hearing that can be very useful if they wear good hearing aids.

sign language There are deaf people all over the world who use sign language. It is a proper language, just like English. The difference is that hand movements and facial expressions are used instead of spoken language. It can't be heard or written. Deaf people use it to talk about everything, just as hearing people use speech.

sign language interpreter An interpreter translates one language into another so that people who use different languages can understand each other. Sign language interpreters turn speech into sign language and sign language into speech to help hearing people and deaf people understand each other.

subtitles A written version of the words and sounds on a television programme or video.

textphone A special telephone with a keyboard and a small screen. Deaf people type in a message and send it to someone else's textphone.

translate To read something in one language and change it into another language.

Typetalk A telephone service that lets hearing people and deaf people talk to each other. A telephone operator reads out a message which the deaf person has typed on a textphone. The operator also types out the hearing person's spoken words for the deaf person to read.

vibrate To move to and fro. Sounds vibrate inside the ear. Vibrations from loud noises can be felt through your body.

Useful addresses

Here are some addresses you can write to for more information about deafness.

Breakthrough Deaf Hearing Integration
(a charity that aims to integrate deaf and hearing people)
Alan Geale House, The Close, Westhill Campus, Bristol Road, Selly Oak, Birmingham B29 6LN

British Deaf Association
(an organization for deaf people who use British Sign Language)
1-3 Worship Street, London EC2A 2AB

HiP Magazine
(a lively magazine for deaf and hearing children, with additional teachers' notes)
1563 Solano Avenue #137, Berkeley, CA 94707, USA

Hearing Dogs for Deaf People
(a charity that trains dogs to alert severely or profoundly deaf people to everyday sounds)
The Training Centre, London Road, Lewknor, Oxon OX9 5RY

The National Deaf Children's Society
(the leading UK charity working with deaf children and their families)
15 Dufferin Street, London EC1Y

The Royal National Institute for Deaf People (RNID)
(the UK's largest charity for deaf people which provides services and campaigns on their behalf)
19-23 Featherstone Street, London EC1Y 8SL

SENSE: The National Deafblind and Rubella Association
(a charity that provides help for deafblind people and their families or carers)
11-13 Clifton Terrace, London N4 3SR

Index